Happy reading, Janet,
Christmas 23

To a dear friend

Tony Barry

# BEES
## Poems That Rhyme

Tony Berry

Copyright © 2023 Tony Berry

All rights reserved.

ISBN 9798850207595

Printed and bound in Great Britain
By Kindle Direct Publishing.

## Forward

Within these pages are poems that I hope are straightforward in manner and easy to read. In their creation I thank my local writers' group for their insightful comments and encouragement. My wife Sheila has read them all and in similar manner the drafts were improved. All mistakes, of course, are my own.

Tony Berry   Northampton   June 2023.

# Contents

| | |
|---|---|
| The Writers Group | 1 |
| Sky, Twitter Netflix et al | 1 |
| It's very strange | 2 |
| Neighbours | 4 |
| Preparations for the 6$^{th}$ of May | 5 |
| Unhappy cycle | 7 |
| Agatha | 8 |
| Where is the good life? | 11 |
| Bees | 11 |
| Growing a little older | 12 |
| Where we are now | 13 |
| A gift from time | 14 |
| Madelaine | 15 |
| The Grand Tour | 16 |
| Almost correct | 17 |
| The Messenger | 18 |
| Alec | 20 |
| Silver | 21 |
| A Summer's afternoon with friends | 22 |
| Tribes | 23 |
| What Women want | 24 |
| Sheila | 24 |
| How others live | 25 |
| A grand Occasion | 26 |
| Leaving the room (1) | 27 |
| The dangers of soccer | 27 |
| Always there | 29 |
| Leaving the room (2) | 29 |
| The clarinettist | 30 |
| The Gardens | 31 |

## The Writers' Group

When muses come and must be told
And authors seek to find a stage,
Holding hard and being bold
With courage firm to turn the page.
A simple smile, a willing face
Will help along the stumbling words.
No mockery, Oh not a trace,
And they will sing as with the birds.
When all is done and rhymes are framed.
The story told and understood.
Spirits return though body still drained.
His task is done as well he could.
Where best to share your feelings true
Than with those who write like you.


## Sky, Twitter, Netflix et al.

In times of your and my grandfather,
Two broadcasters met all our needs,
Family programmes mixed with laughter,
News, politics and sporting deeds.
Both tended a single community.
All discourse was common to all.
In the two we found our unity,
We were blind to our coming fall.
Internet, technology. Oh! How we loved the choice.
Now we are individuals, there is no common voice.
Reaching for the future, all warnings we did flout.
There is no one else to blame. We let the Genie out.

## It's Very Strange

Said Tweedledum to Tweedledee,
"I've got some marvellous news.
In all matters Tweedleish
We've got the right to choose.
In the morning I'll be dum
And in the afternoon be dee
And you can, if you wish,
Be the opposite of me."

"There's no such thing as opposite,"
Said the Red Queen in her spite.
"Each and every one of us
Can just be who we like."

The White Rabbit cried,
"I have been investigated.
It seems as yet
I'm not fully integrated."
He still does not understand
His catalogue of crimes,
Bequeathed by his forebears
From past colonial times.

The Cheshire Cat appeared,
Upset by all the chatter
And claimed to have forgotten,
Whose lives really matter?
"I'm a disappearing expert
But even I would falter
At making certain statues
Disappear into the water."

The Mad Hatter spoke
With great lucidity
On mortifying problems
With his university.
"They keep putting books
On shelves beyond my reach.
I have to be protected
From something called free speech."

Said the March Hare
As he lay upon the road,
"Climate change requires
I am very, very bold.
Obstructing others
Is a March Hare's right.
Idiot deniers
Deserve a heavy fright.
It is so jolly good
That our judges do agree
And none in this land
Will ever sentence me."

The soft, furry dormouse
Into the teapot curled.
Preferring to live
In her own special world.
The Red King complained,
His voice all confusion,
That people say,
"We are the illusion."

The friends of Lewis Carroll,
In their rather silly way,
Are warning us, "Be careful
What you do and what you say."
For there are snarks about
Chanting out in rote
Rules and laws and punishments
For those who never WOKE.


## In Praise of Neighbours

Our son is entering retirement,
Our memories a failing power,
Physical strength and energy spent,
Grandchildren stay but an hour.
Tentatively facing each new day,
There are those half-felt by our side,
Who cross garden and terrace And roadway
Ensure, "Yes! They have not yet died."
Families once stayed to support you,
As did friends of an earlier date.
Now kith and kin have their lives to pursue
And friends share our pressing fate.
Best as we can we continue our labours,
Safe in the help and the care of our neighbours.

# Preparations for May 6th 2023

We are going up to London,
To see the new king crowned.
We have had a look together
And a viewpoint we have found.
Mother, father, auntie
Insist they come with us,
They have tickets for the train,
Brollies for the rain,
And the number of the bus.

We are getting there early
Awaiting of the dawn,
With folding chairs and thermos
And blankets nice and warm.
It was with heavy heart
We left the dog at home.
He is staying with a neighbour,
On his best behaviour,
But he's got his favourite bone.

We shall sit down, comfort like,
Awaiting for the bands.
Sharing from our Tupperware
With folk from foreign lands.
We have given much thought
To the question of our fare.
We have rolls mainly ham,
Scones with cream and jam,
All made with loving care.

There was one important matter
On which father would not waver.
He expected from us all
Our very best behaviour.
Oh! such strictures were severe
When the king was drawing near.
If we had songs, we should sing,
Bells we should ring,
And give the King a cheer.

So, we are ready to go
But we think you ought to know
That the last event like this
Happened many years ago.
And you will grind your teeth in doubt,
If you think that you've missed out.
Just get out of your chair,
hurry on down there,
and give the pair a shout.

# An Unhappy Cycle

The Dictator is overthrown,
His long reign has come to an end.
He and his family have fled abroad,
A life of riches, always bored,
No one's really best friend.

The people dance in the streets.
New elections will surely be called.
Law and justice will soon revive.
Peace and prosperity will grow and thrive
And a new leader is gracefully installed.

A fresh government is swiftly formed.
International loans agreed.
Political exiles are welcomed back home,
Gulag prisoners released to roam,
All critical journalists freed.

Alas, early mistakes are made,
Some groups left out in the cold.
But the Army enjoys its new guns and tanks,
For the Secret Police more pay for all ranks,
And the Media is fully controlled.

Through unforeseen technical problems,
The elections must now be delayed.
Arrests are due for a troublesome few.
Church and Unions told what to do,
And new judges have to be made.

Opposition is out in the open,
The cry "To the barricades!"
Students are throwing their Molotov cocktails,
Farmers, blocking the roads with their hay bales.
All law and order fades.

At a time of such social breakdown,
"Bring us stability," the public urges.
There is only one course,
The man on the white horse,
At last, a new General emerges.

## Agatha

Oh! I do love Agatha Christie,
She always seems to please.
She gives us a difficult mystery,
But one we can read with ease.
I feel at home in her library,
The vicar in his church,
The colonel with a dodgy past,
And the young man left in the lurch.
The country house and the seaside town
And the once well-known hotel,
The speeding train and the sinister boat
And the village called Dingley Dell.

Once inside this special place,
At at a specific time
I'm introduced to the heart of the matter,
A rather gruesome crime.
In this there are no favourites,
Decease comes in many ways.
Some are rather ordinary
But others still amaze.
The poison draught, the far- off shot,
The blow to the head, the unpleasant garrotte,
The knife in the dark, the suspicious fall,
One way or another she covers them all.

Early in our discourse,
Oh! What are we to do?
Then comes the famous sleuth,
Always one of two.
My favourite is Miss Marple,
A kindly spinster lady,
Who quietly sits and quietly knits
And ponders matters gravely.
The culprits overlook her,
so thoughtful in repose.
But she is their nemesis
And thus, they are exposed.

The second of our sleuths
Is one you are sure to know.
He goes by the foreign name
Of Hercule Poirot.
He is a slight of stature Belgian,
but as Agatha tells,
He is a rather good detective,
Having little grey cells,

And when he finally gets them,
A-working overtime,
It seems that he can solve
Just any sort of crime.

Each case requires
A Scotland Yard detective,
Who from the beginning
Is rather ineffective.
He ignores the hints and help
From our famous two.
He wanders around in circles,
Never knowing what to do.
At last the penny drops
And to their views he does attest,
And finally we observe
A most welcome arrest.

And when the bad guys are locked up
And the jewellery back in place,
The secret plans returned
And no one in disgrace,
When everything is clear
And not a wistful mystery,
We shall never meet
But we sit at the feet
Of the wonderful Agatha Christie.

## Where is the Good Life?

Cathedral, grammar school, cricket and choir
Good places where decent folk prosper.
Where we can live our middle-class lives,
Where all of us look like each other.
The city edge golf club where royalty played
Is open and easy to enter.
The volunteer theatre down by the parade
Gives us Shakespeare and Arnold Wesker.
Holiday villas a boat at Port Bou restores
Our inner well-being.
And if the dividends keep up this year,
There will be just enough for some skiing.
Blessed by the sea, a yacht club for some
Keeps landsmen and children at bay.
The churches all thrive and the bishops at home,
And God's in his heaven all day.

## Bees

On each day I like to see
The honest, English worker bee.
I always like to check his flight
To see that he has got it right.
For bees are known to be such charmers,
They always fool the silly farmers,
Who spend a great deal of their lives
Making bees their special hives,
Thinking bees and their honey
Will bring them piles and piles of money.
But for bees, honey is no loss.
They really see it as just dross,
And what the farmers do not see,
Is all the bees just live rent free.

## Growing a Little Older

"It's macular degeneration" the surgeon said
And he gave a wintry smile.
I quietly sat and quietly thought
And was quiet for quite a while.
"Well! What exactly is it?"
I asked of the medical sage.
"Oh! Nothing at all to worry about.
It's all to do with your age."
"I'm only forty- two," I said,
"It seems so very unfair."
"It's the world we live in," he replied,
"The world of wear and tear."

"You'll need eye injections," he added,
Looking rather more grave.
"It's all to do with the back of the eye,
The bit we are trying to save."
I thought about it long and hard,
But really it was no surprise.
It's absolutely essential,
That you always look after your eyes.

And so, the first day, of many to come,
And to the clinic I trudged.
Holding hard my rising fears
And knowing my courage to be judged.


The smiling nurse seemed happy to see me,
She told me where to sit.
And then it was drops and drops and drops
And some burnt quite a bit.

Then lying before the surgeon,
I was ready for any measure.
Some gauze on the face, a clip into place
And  then a little pressure.
Lying there waiting, I suggested
He might want to begin.
Instead, he turned away from me.
"The injection has already gone in. "

Well! what a delight, the world was bright.
"Was it really as easy as this?"
My heart all a-beat, I got to my feet,
The nurse just missing a kiss.
So now we finish the poem
And at last we come to the twist.
I would rather an eye injection,
Than the work of the finest dentist.

## Where we are Now

The Barbarian from the East
Living in past time said,
"Ukraine is mine."
There will be no peace.
On your lands I will feast.
Your young men will die.
Sisters will cry.
For babies unborn,
Mothers will morn.

The Peoples of the West,
Had not taken note.
They had clung to false hope.
But now they knew best.
There would be no more rest.
All was sharp clear.
Now cast-off dull fear.
No longer innocence forsaken,
But with confidence unshaken,
Support for a nation,
Whose land had been taken.


## A gift from time

It was many years before we met,
Wise, unwise our personal histories.
Lives lived long without regret,
Searching for new mysteries.
Madelaine knows she has my heart,
I, a fair friend not a fairy's lure,
A natural man not framed by art,
Passions real for ever sure.
Collapse defence, face full the risk.
Staid! Staid! Grasp the hour.
Bravely take that lingering kiss,
Feel nature's pulsing power.
Come make full love our own success,
Madelaine, Madelaine, Madelaine, say yes.

## Madelaine

Your loving words that are so fine,
You full believe them at the time,
But men will find such words with ease,
Perhaps well-meaning but still deceive.
It's fine to hear such words so tender,
But man is nature's great dissembler.
Yes, you say I have your heart,
In truth it is a little part.
I would rather know the man.
Have I a lion or a lamb?
Is he kind? Is he forgiving?
Has he coin for two hearts living?
Has he patience? Can he trust?
How does he balance love and lust?
Rather than those words of rhyme,
I would you offered of your time.
It's time not words I wish from you,
When two one's would be as two.
Fair friend for you a sad blow.
Madelaine, she answers NO.

# The Grand Tour

A journey twenty years ago still fills my mind with awe.
I wandered from Byzantium along Aegean's shore.
Crossing the Hellespont, I pondered Troy's distress,
Then up to high Pergamum and sea-flanked Ephesus.
I felt the world of grandeur, the proof of man's ascent,
But from those sad, dark ruins came a different testament.
The wise men who ruled those days had mastered much of life,
But even in their small world had not kept man from strife.

At Antioch, Aleppo, I sensed a change of tone
With fine semitic warriors, crusaders from Rome.
Kings and Caliphs thronged the desert stage
But fighting face to face with ever-growing rage.
The horizons of those times were wider than of yore
But still there was death, from weapons of war.

So out past Stylite's seat to Damascus on the plain,
Where armies vainly struggled to seek eternal fame
And rifle butt and bayonet sharp and master of the sea
Finally reached exhausted, its imperial apogee.
The wise men made their treaties. "So many men to please."
They thought map and boundary line would solve disputes with ease.
But answers in Paris that looked so very sound
Rarely solved the problems when laid out on the ground.

Then came into my mind the famous Balfour draft,
Promising a country based upon the past.
A very special country modern and new,
A firm and final homeland for the ever-wandering jew.
I turned to find some hope in the much-divided city,
Where wall and dome both had claims to empathy and pity,
To grow a special place of love and peace and wonder.
But no! They chose to split the world and render it asunder.

As I left behind the Golden Gate and came down from the hill,
My constant thought kept telling me, "How easy men do kill."
And now they have great sponsors who tell them they are right,
Involving us all in their long and bloody fight.
So, what new rule has history placed upon my brow,
To better guide me through our later life?
The answer is unpleasant but we must face it now.
Man's fate is one of everlasting strife.

## Almost Correct

Those who tell us of our weather have a very tricky task,
A Kingdom to survey within oceans so vast.
They study so intensely their meteorology,
That's chemistry and physics and polyologies.
They worry all the time, on sun and wind and rain
And that so much of our land is simply not the same.
So, Dover may be wet and Doncaster dry,
But Bristol very sunny with high clouds in the sky.
It's a wonder they manage to cover us at all,
From Orkney to the Scillies and Fife to Rockall.
But there is a group of eight million and I think it quite a shame,
That weather men and women rarely mention their name.
It may be a small issue, but it is one to ponder on.
It's a place in the South-East, that folk there, call London.
Perhaps in the future a mention they could make
Of weather information, for when the Londoners awake.

# The Messenger
## (A pastiche of *The Listeners* by Walter De La Mare)

"Is there anybody there?" said the messenger,
As again he pressed the bell,
But all he heard was the wailing wind
Across the icy fell.
And the mountains looked down upon him
As he struggled with his task.
And he rang the bell a third time.
"Is there anyone there?" he asked.
But there was no light from within
As he peered through the door,
Feeling that silent winter
And its day so sharp and raw.
Then he heard the scratching,
The scumberling as from a den,
Hidden shapes and furry noise
Inimical to men.
There in the failing daylight
He felt exposed and alone,
Grudging of the duty
That kept him from his home.
Then in the stillness
He heard a feeble cry,
Of a different timbre
To the seagulls in the sky.
Now he strongly shouted
And beat upon the door,
Searching through the casement,
A body on the floor.
All doubt left him.
He knew for heaven's sake,
Inside this house

Was the one man left awake.
And an icy panic gripped him
As he looked about for aid,
But all that was there was a road to the West
With the light beginning to fade.
At last, he found his courage
And made the emergency call.
With name, number and reference, he told them of it all.
And he found he could breathe again,
At the thought of those coming to assist.
And his mind returned to the man again,
The man he had almost missed.
But soon in the distance,
He heard the siren's wail
And he began framing the words
For the telling of his tale.
And when all was done
And all authority pleased,
They praised him and thanked him
And allowed him then to leave.
So the tired messenger, who had
So well completed his quest,
Turned on the engine of his van
And drove off into the West.
It seems that the official police work
Was something of a mess.
For however hard anyone tried,
They never found out his address.

# Alec

The colonel so fraught in the jungle's strong heat,
The man in the white suit, so sartorially neat,
The sheik in the desert no less a King,
A man called Smiley with his clever spy ring.
Some of the roles that this actor has played;
There on the screen his talents displayed.
The doctor so serious and dear Father Brown,
The Lavender Hill Mob, was it Coronet and Crown?
Of ordinary stature, a plain looking face,
A light touch of make-up, but only a trace.
There before us a change so profound,
A different character to amaze and astound.
The Man from Havana with his moral choice,
Great Expectations with that light piping voice,
The warrior in Star Wars and Ebeneezer Scrooge,
Which is the finest? So difficult to choose.
A collection of work that time will not diminish,
A full life's endeavour from Sir Alec Guinness.
The actors' actor led his profession.
Now he is gone, I see no succession.

# Silver

Silver comes from the ground much easier than gold.
It has a similar story, one equally as bold.
Some history linked to silver is not of the best.
Silver tongues and silver spoons are concepts better left.
There's the thirty pieces of silver for which we have our shame,
Even though it was Judas that should bear all the blame.
But polished silver shines and gleams, a joy for all our eyes.
Visual treasures to behold each piece so highly prized;
Napkin rings, mustard pots, cruets by the score,
Cream jugs, sporting cups and many, many more.
Silver is the people's choice, our little bit of wealth.
Often, we neglect it and leave it on the shelf.
But if we take it down and with soft rags make it gleam,
It always repays us with a burning bright sheen.
Silver is for artists to show off all their skills,
With frog, feather, and filigree and fruit and flora frills.
And when we have admired each plate and bowl and ladle,
We can turn our minds to a special type of table.
With date stamp and maker's mark we travel back in time
To meet our finest silversmiths working in their prime.
We see their name so clearly it fills our minds with trust
For quality and value, it is for such things that we lust.
So, if you have some silver, don't hide it right away,
It's survived any plot for the melting pot, and should be on display.

## A Summer's Afternoon With Friends

I've walked many paths in my county, both dry and water-logged miles,
Aided by those countryside features of stepping stones, signposts and stiles.
Normally, such outdoor pursuits involve others desiring to roam,
But on this particular occasion, I would venture out on my own.
I knew of a special valley, I had chosen it with care.
Its isolation hinted that some rare, loved friends were there.
A thick set wood with a grassy path beckoned me along,
I felt the health of nature the browns and greens so strong.
The air so warm, I breathed in deep the smell of fern and tree.
That path, indeed, had brought me close to the friends I longed to see.
Gatekeeper, Speckled Wood danced with Meadow Brown
With Brimstone and Peacock high up in the crown.

All through the day I watched friends at play
Whispering in and out the shadows.
Fluttering and gliding in acrobatic ways,
Dodging bushes and their gloomy hallows.
On my bare arms, rested a fine Painted Lady,
While Holly Blue and Orange Tip tripped around me gaily.
Forever in my glance, how merrily they danced,
Wings of colour so delicate and fine.
I really must say, a momentous day,
A moment of life so sublime.
As I sat late, my friends chose their fate
And spent their life's hours there with me.
I hated that thought that the waning day brought
And lost my tranquillity.
As the dusk tiptoed in, came the day's reckoning
And I found myself standing alone.
I had seen the display of butterflies at play,
The moment was here to go on home.

I have retraced my steps to that valley,
Hoping those self-same friends to find,
But you will be sorry to hear that year after year,
Nature was never so kind.

## Tribes

Some fair English towns still have tribes,
Bounded by avenue and street,
Stiffly living their separate lives,
Observing, not caring to meet.
Trimmed hedges, spy cameras
and shaven lawns, sit nicely with Julie and Michael.
Whilst Mick, Steve and pretty Shavaughn
Have backyards, broken prams, a broken cycle.
Ballet classes, bridge, weekends at Le Mans
Try to keep ennui away.
Whilst job seekers, sick note, and work humdrum
Might just keep the bailiffs at bay.
Fear stalks one tribe, envy the other.
Never at peace, they just mutter and mutter.

## What women want

When he said he respected her,
She sniffed.
When he said he admired her,
She smiled.
When he said he adored her,
She laughed.
When he said he worshipped her,
She groaned.
When he said he loved her,
She was his.


## Sheila

The truest friend I have in life
I'm proud to say it is my wife.
Quiet composed in every way,
A calming presence through the day.
Yet full of fun and life's great joys,
An artisan, yet full of poise.
A source of love that burns so bright,
A comfort through the darkest night.
Sought out by those whose lives are fraught,
Each time she gives warm care, cool thought.
A life of music and of books,
Favoured by nature to keep her looks.
I hope in time the world will see,
I am to her as she to me.

## How Others Live

A sad day may arrive when you can no longer drive.
How sad and cross you suddenly become,
And the resulting lot of fuss means you have to take the bus,
And from this monumental change you cannot hide.
Now the first part of this plot is to find the right bus stop.
It may well mean standing in the rain.
There may well be a queue but that must not worry you,
For you will learn to stay within the flock.
When you are safe and sound inside, looking forward to your ride,
There are rules of combat you'll do well to learn
Do not smile, do not frown, just keep on looking down
And this way you are likely to survive.
Staying with this theme, there is more to be seen.
But you must learn to take it in your stride.
Babies mewl and cry, gropers on the sly
And other folk not so very clean.
And when the journey's done and the race, run and won,
With the big red bus your normal way to travel.
People from another place have grown to know your face
And you'll say travelling in this way is really fun.

# A Grand Occasion

Each country of the world promotes their special dish.
Many from the finest meat or from the freshest fish.
The English love to eat such fayre with a genuine satisfaction,
But there is also a native dish that remains a great attraction.
It is the only dish of which an Englishman may boast,
The wildly glorious, life-enhancing English Sunday roast.
The whole grand occasion is really like no other,
For all secrets are passed down to daughter from mother.
Try to be a guest at someone else's table,
Where expertise abounds, never a shop label.
It will have been prepared for many happy years,
Always successful without any tears.
There is a certain etiquette you must be sure to master.
There is never a desert and certainly no starter.
Also avoid or you will pay a price,
On entering the kitchen to give some good advice.
And when the magic's done and all are in their place,
Remember such occasions often start with a grace.
Then stay strong and silent holding of your nerve
And with any luck you will be the first one served.
Meat soft and tender, potatoes dark and brown,
Vegetables firm all waiting for the crown
Of high Yorkshire pudding, hot, light and tasty,
Awaiting the anointment of the all-important gravy.
And when you are replete and fighting of the sleep
Thinking of the bits enjoyed the most.
Although it's always handy, please avoid the brandy.
Just leave with many thanks to your host.

## Leaving the room (1)

Some say old age is a war fought on many fronts,
A hard daily struggle when years shrink to months.
Health, wealth and happiness on each you take a stand,
Full prescriptions, blood tests, injections carefully planned.
Anxiously you view those like you who finally reach their journey's end.
Then a review, with information new, tells you are clearly on the mend.
You look with hopeless envy on those with private care,
That's a financial burden you simply cannot bear.
You mutter about state provision, appointments cancelled or lost.
The General Practice receptionist, the one like Mother Frost.
You fight off resignation you grimly stick to your task.
Sons and daughters required to help, it's their turn at last.
Then you face the final moment, you hear the words so tender.
It's time to go, you really know, but by God you will not surrender.

## The Dangers Of Soccer

You can go and change your house,
You can go and change your bank,
In your dreams you can even change your wife.
But there is a sporting choice
That as man and boy you'll voice,
That will certainly last you all your life.

It is from a wide selection
That you make this key election,
Which soccer team you wish to make your own.
It's rarely very rational,
Even contra-fashionable
And bound to make your many friends groan.

At the pub when playing pool,
Where the girls all think you are cool,
You strut about with scarf and shirt so chic.
But it's not so very funny
When you count the sort of money
This team of yours is costing every week.

Likely you will become a bore,
Always asking for the score,
As the fortunes of your team wax and wane.
And when you meet a fellow fan,
Who is clearly from your clan,
Your superiority you both will hotly claim.

As a fan you need success,
Victories to excess,
Trophies and medals in great number.
If your team gets it right,
To your constant delight,
Other fans of other teams, in envy, wonder.

There is danger with this fun
That you become a hooligan,
Bare-chested singing out a loathsome song.
Marching with a mob
You become a silly yob,
Losing all sense of right and wrong.

The reality my friend
Is that right up to the end,
This choice of yours has been an utter folly.
I think that it is true
That the best thing you can do
Is find, this time, a much more worthwhile hobby.

## Always there

When days are cold and nights are chill
And frost and snow engulf us all,
When cars can't start and trains are still
And pensioners begin to fall,
When post and parcel do not move
And modern ferries stay in dock
And latch-key kids can't go to school,
For ice has frozen key and lock
Who through action and real grit
Struggle on to do their bit?
It's boys and girls who with their labours,
Bring each day our morning papers.
We poor things seek to be warmer,
When heroes come from round the corner.

## Leaving the room (2)

Managing your final years has much to do with time.
For some a kindly doctor sets the date.
For others it's a state of mind, "I hope it will be mine"
To accept the nature of our fate.
Such clarity restores control, you manage your own life,
And there will be much that stays the same,
But now you are on a journey, no more a state of strife
Making choices as your powers wane.
Dealing with visitors is hard but you will cope,
You choose what you eat and where you sit.
Family and friends pour out their false hope,

But you ignore it every little bit.
You can still explore new things and go to bed when you like.
TV and tablet at your command,
Drinking whisky, smoking fags, playing bingo every night,
And watching dodgy films from foreign lands.
While you like to sleep a lot, awake you grow benign,
A quieter life, exempt from every chore.
You suffer tepid baths rooting out the grime,
That part you find a ghastly bore.
When you never leave your bed and the whispering starts to come,
And you value every loving touch.
You will turn to everyone. They will know when you are done,
And just say, "Thank you very much."


## The Clarinettist

Nature's law is firmly set, that to play the clarinet
You must begin to play before the age of nine.
But for those aged twenty-three, the sad reality
Is that you simply do not have enough of time.
It was not a crazy bet that led you to the clarinet,
Rather the gentle prodding of your wife.
So, taking matters in hand, you went and joined a band
And that is how music became your life.
Now just as you are moving on there is a problem troublesome.
The cognoscenti name it as "the bridge".
Fingers flying from a G hopefully grasping for that B,
It really is a nasty edge.
Still early progress was quite good, you changed from plastic to wood,
And a part-time tutor was eventually hired.
With a fine ex-bandsman soldier, you started getting bolder,

But fingers, back and neck were getting tired.
He said "Now here are some helpful tips. It is all about the lips
And he made me change my embouchure.
"Then if scales you can cram and control your diaphragm,
All your notes will come out sounding pure."
Then that marvellous year when you found your musical ear.
No longer do you need to read the score.
When they hear how good you are with an expanded repertoire,
Impresarios come knocking at your door.
That life of practice you accepted meant temptations all rejected,
That the level "maestro" became your mission.
Twelve hours every day, for twenty years they say
And, finally, you've reached your life's ambition.
The naysayers were dumfounded, your family quite astounded.
This skill will serve you all your life.
You can charge any fee as a music celebrity
And this has proved the wisdom of your wife.

## The Gardens

Our house has two gardens each with a different role.
The front is carefully managed, the back just grows and grows.
Not quite a fortress, the front's a public space.
The back meets our family needs, a very private place

The flowers at the front are those that come and go,
Snow drops, blue bells and daffodils all aglow.
White, blue and yellow are the colours that they bring,
Such a delight, such harbingers of spring.

With low stone wall, sharp cut hedge, both a smoke and a magnolia tree,
A well swept drive and a shaven lawn says "welcome to 23".
A row of well-placed tubs, offer more expensive flora,

And carefully placed waste bins are hidden around the corner.

Her summer dress is indeed the best for the private garden.
Sounds and scents and colour too make up her royal diadem.
Humming bees and swaying trees, light sounds that can be heard.
Then sweetly singing, sweetly trilling songs of garden birds.

Lavender and orange blossom pass on scents divine,
With honeysuckle, lilac and climbing columbine.
Here there is a canvas of many shades of green,
Sprouting and melding in line with nature's scheme.

The flowers there so rich with reds and whites and cream,
A palette of colour, every painter's dream.
Squirrels and hedgehogs, a rather scruffy fox,
Are for us pleasing, regular sights,
While dragonflies and butterflies, in their own time,
enjoy their many mazy flights.

At the end of this garden is a very special place,
A small pond, a few logs: there is very little space.
But if we are quiet and can avoid the nettles,
We will see how our frogs and newts very gently settle.

Through summer shine and winter snow the front we do control,
But whose hand controls the back, I really do not know.

Printed in Great Britain
by Amazon